HARVEY CIRCLE

HARVEY CIRCLE

MARY E. HINES

authorHOUSE®

AuthorHouse™
1663 Liberty Drive
Bloomington, IN 47403
www.authorhouse.com
Phone: 1-800-839-8640

Published by AuthorHouse   06/07/2012

ISBN: 978-1-4772-0742-0 (sc)
ISBN: 978-1-4772-0741-3 (e)

Library of Congress Control Number: 2012909186

Any people depicted in stock imagery provided by Thinkstock are models, and such images are being used for illustrative purposes only.
Certain stock imagery © Thinkstock.

This book is printed on acid-free paper.

Because of the dynamic nature of the Internet, any web addresses or links contained in this book may have changed since publication and may no longer be valid. The views expressed in this work are solely those of the author and do not necessarily reflect the views of the publisher, and the publisher hereby disclaims any responsibility for them.

CONTENTS

PREFACE

Walter and Emma Mae Harvey

We share with you the life of two lovely people, WALTER and EMMA MAE HARVEY. We are very happy to share their contributions, success, outstanding achievements, and the fruits of their labor. We hope that your hearts will be encouraged.

Their love, teaching, sharing, and caring began at home and spreaded throughout their communities and abroad.

ACKNOWLEDGEMENTS

We are eternally grateful for our Christian parents. We are grateful for their unending love and devotion to us. We continue to thank and praise God for this blessing in our life. Our wonderful Christian parents touched each of our life in a special way. We will always honor and love our parents and praise our heavenly father for our Christian parents. Each of us remembers our mother and father and their unconditional love and devotion in our life.

WALTER AND EMMA MAE HARVEY (60) YEARS OF MARRIAGE

WALTER 1910-2007   EMMA MAE 1915-1992

Walter Harvey September 9, 1910-March 15, 2007

Emma Mae Harvey January 24, 1915-April 25, 1992

Walter Harvey and Emma Mae Johnson-Harvey were born in the State of Mississippi. Walter was born to the parents of Walt L. Harvey and Gertrude Washington Harvey in Mississippi Delta. His parents attempted to escape the Delta plantation when he was a baby. The white plantation owners pursued them and overtook them and killed Walter's father and brothers who were traveling together. They threaten to take his life also, but Walter was saved by one of the white men who spoke and said, "Do the baby no harm" and he took him and gave him back to his mother and told them to be on their way.

Walter was one of the (12) twelve children raise by his mother and stepfather Percy Edwards in Bolton, Mississippi. He courted and married Emma Mae Johnson, who was the daughter of Mabel Hill Johnson and Lacy Johnson. She was one of five children, (3 boys and 2 girls). She was (15) fifteen years of age when her mother died. Her father married again to Willie Mae Todd and they had a family, two boys and one girl.

Emma Mae married Walter when she was (17) seventeen years of age. They were the parents of (19) children, six (6) of these that passed from childbirth, to age nine (9). They raise (5) boys and (8) girls one of these (13) children the oldest son Walter Jr. proceeded his parents in death at the age of 50.

Walter and Emma Mae lived West of Bolton, the first few years of life as sharecroppers. They moved East of Bolton and they became landowners. Emma Mae's father, Lacy Johnson bought land from Mary Johnson in the Mt. Olive community, "The old pelts place" and Lacy gave this land (deed) to his daughter and her husband Walter and Emma Mae and their children farmed his land. They raised cattle, horse and hogs. They willed this farm equally to their children.

They became outstanding neighbors in the Mr. Olive community and faithful loyal members of the Mr. Olive church. They were God fearing and taught their children to be God fearing and respectful. Walter was ordained as a Deacon and Emma Mae served on the motherboard of the Mr. Olive church. They taught Sunday school for many years. They held these positions until death.

They were faithful members until their health fail them. Their children were also faithful members attending Sunday school bible classes and pray services also choir members. Their participation was appreciated. Walter, Emma Mae, and their children had great abilities and skills and talent.

Walter was a very good farmer. His crops were always good. He always had a good garden summer and winter. He and Emma Mae always shared their fruits and vegetables with their neighbors far and near. When he killed hogs in the winter he also shared with his neighbors. They made lard from the hogs fat that would last all winter into the summer also the ham would keep well in the smoke houses for many months. The cows were milk, every morning until latter years. There would always be plenty of milk to drink and churned. They made their own butter from churning the creamed milk. They raised peanuts, potatoes, sweet potatoes, tomatoes, greens, onion, peas, beans, okra, corn, sugar cane, and other fruits and vegetables and more. We had fruit tress apple, pears, peach, plum, pecans, and the berries, plenty of black berries and plums during the spring months in and around the pasture.

Walter and the children would always finish chopping and harvesting their crops on time, and became hired labors to the neighbors. During the summer months Walter would work in the city. Emma and the children canned fruits, and vegetables. During harvest months the cotton was picked and bales of cotton was taken to the gin by Walter. He would always return home with fruit and treats for the children. Corn was pluck and put into the barn. Peanuts were plowed up and put on the housetop to dry and stored in Crocker sacks into the storehouse. Sweet potatoes were plowed up and stored unto the potatoes bed made of corn stock and hay. Sugar canes and sorgum cane were gathered and grind into molasses. Peas were gathered and stored unto Crocker sacks. Wood was cut and piled up near the house to heat the stove to cook and burn in the fireplace for heat in the house. Port meat was used for bacon and cooking the vegetables. The hens laid eggs most of the year. The chickens were fed during the winter months everyday so were the dogs, and the hogs. Water was drawn from the well every day and the house was kept clean every day.

The children had pets. They had pets cats, dogs, hogs, chicken, a goat, a calf and even a horse.

They learn to ride the horse at an early age. They did chores every evening. The dogs were fed, the chickens were fed, the hogs were fed and the cows were separated from the calves. The cows were milk in the morning; the wood was cut and brought into the house. The clothes were washed, hung and dried often. The yard was swept in the spring and summer.

The early days transportation was done by walking, riding the horse or mule in a wagon or the neighbor's car. In 1948, Walter and Emma Mae bought their first car. The family no longer had to walk or hick a ride.

Walter loved to hunt during the winter month. His bothers-in-law lived in Chicago. They would come down and hunt during the winter months mostly they killed rabbits, quails, squirrels and ducks. They would start hunting early in the morning and return when they got tired or late in the evening. Their dog (the bird dog, a setter) would be tired too. Emma's bothers usually left the dog behind with the children. We always welcome Emma's brothers whenever they came to visit. They would always bring her money and the girls too.

The old fashion iron was used to iron with. It was made of iron. Kerosene was used in lamps for light. The iron stove was used to cook on or cook in. It was made of iron and heated by using wood. The iron was heated on the stove or by the hot coals of fire in the fireplace. Starch was made from a mixture of flour and water to starch clothes. Sometimes peanuts and potatoes were cook on the fireplace. The family would sit around the fireplace on a cold night doing homework or laughing and talking or reading the bible.

When electricity reached the rural area in the fifths, most everything was changed for the best. The iron became less of a problem so did the stove. Mama bought her first old-fashion washing machine. We still had to fill the washing machine with water and it had a hand wringer. The washboard was no longer needed. The tub was still used to take a bath in and help with the clothes washed. The old slop pot was used until the toilet came into use. The face pan was used to wash in long after the face bowel was put into the house. The clothes were still washed and hung outside to dry. In the summer time the clothes would soon dried by the warm or hot sun. The clothes were hung on the clothes line made from a string of wire or straight wire by the older children.

Walter and Emma Mae knew where their children were at all times. If they went to a neighbor's house or went someplace with someone their children had to have permission to leave the house at all time unless they sent them some place. The children had to be in the house early every night. If they went socializing they had to be back by nine o clock. They were allowed to visit on the weekend. On Sunday everyone went to church. Some Saturday they went to Bolton with their parents. Boys were not allowed to visit the house when the parents were not home.

In 1959, 1960 or 1961, the gravel road was paved from Bolton to Hwy49 in Jackson and it became Northside Drive. The Rural route name was changed to honor those citizens in the community. Our address was changed to Harvey Circle from route 2, Walter and Emma Mae had a new three bedroom house built and moved into it the year of 1988, Sandra, the youngest child, was married in the new house in 1990.

Walter made sure his family got to Sunday school and church service on time He took his children to Sunday school. He carried all the babies in his arm before he had a car. He would always look out for his family. He would support his family. He loved his wife and children and he did his best to provide for them. He called his wife "Baby" all the time He kept a garden all the year and chicken to eat all the year. He loved to farm. He was always chopping or cutting weeds around the house or in the field. He loved to smoke his cigars or just hold them in his mouth. He could be heard humming a song often. He also would sing early in the morning as he did his chores feeding the dogs or the hogs. One of his favorite songs was "Glory Glory halleluiah" since I laid my burdens down". At church he loved to take charge of or participate in devotion. He was an on time man he was never late. He was a count on me person (dedicated). He supported the children schools faithfully. His favorite hymns were "Jesus keep me near the cross" and "father I stretch my hand to thee". His favorite scriptures were St. John 14:1-10 and 1st Psalm. His advices and sharing scripture was proverbs 3:5,6 "Lean not to thy own understanding in all thy ways acknowledge him and he shall direct your path". When he got sick, he said to his children "Do the right thing". His motto was; Do unto others as you would have them do unto you".

Walter always blessed the food and the children said a verse as he and family sat at the table to eat breakfast, dinner and supper. Emma Mae was a loving sharing and caring person. She was very clean. No one came to her house hungry and left hungry if she knew you were hungry she feed you. She was very intelligent a very good mother and a very clean person. She would say "I know every one of my children as to their character". She was a very good cook and taught her girls to cook. Wash, iron and clean the house. She was an educator. She would see to it that you learn your lessons and helped with everyone's homework. She was interested in everyone's lesson and made sure everyone kept up with what they were supposed to do. She supported her children in school and supported the school also. She went to school for her children if there was a problem. She went to Sunday school with the family, she taught Sunday school and she formed and directed the youth choir. She cooked three meals a day especially breakfast and dinner. Many times supper was the same as dinner. The family loved to eat milk and bread for supper.

The family ate well and healthy. Vegetables were raised all year, certain vegetables in summer and certain vegetables in winter. Tomatoes, peas, onion, okra, beans squash, and melons were plentiful in their season.

Most morning we were awaken to the aroma of bake biscuits, bacon, coffee and hot butter grits. Emma Mae would do breakfast early and Walter would help her. They were a good team. They were very agreeable.

Emma Mae would make cakes, pies and cookies regularly. Every holiday, she always cooked plenty of food to eat for the family and relatives who always came to visit. Emma Mae was the business person in the family. She knew math well and she did not allow anyone to cheat her or her husband. She would keep the oldest children clothes or shoes and give it to the next child. She would sew and make dresses for her girls. She did such a good job that she continues to make clothes for some of them when they were grown-ups. She was her children's beautician and sometimes the neighbor's beautician. She loved children and kept many of her grand children. They all loved her and called her Mama Emma. She was dedicated to her husband and children and faithful to the church. She attended to Baptism services as well as Holy Communion services; she made the wine and bread for the church services on many occasions. She could quilt and many times had the neighbor\s mothers to meet at her house to quilt in the winter months. She taught her girls to sew. She had an old fashion iron singer sewing machine. She was always a good wife a very good mother. She was a good neighbor. She was a sweet person all about sharing and caring. Her favorite song was "precious Lord take my hand". She knew many songs. She could be heard singing or humming songs even when she got sick. She did not complaint. She new bible verses and scriptures and would remind you of what the Bible said, she was our beloved mother, our friend, and we all loved her. She was blessed with wisdom, plenty of "mother wit" and a six sense. The scripture that describe her best is proverbs 31:10-31

She attended to the sick in the community. Their children were seldom sick. When the children had a stomach ache, they gave them soda water. When the children had a cold she gave them castor oil. When they were not doing too well, she gave them cod liver oil. She made every one comfortable when you had the measles, mumps or chicken pox or even a boil she knew how to treat everything. Her presence made you feel better even when you had a headache. Her love for you helped to make it better. No matter what the problem was. If one had a bad cold, or fever, Emma Mae would go seeking for ginseng weed. She got them, and boil them and made tea and gave it to the sick person. They seldom went to the doctor, over all they were healthy people. Everyone always came to the table to eat at the appropriate breakfast, dinner and supper.

There was never a curse word said in the house. The Bible was often studied and bible verses memorized. The children gave honor and respect to their parents and adults. Spiritual songs were heard and song in the home. Their children were educated and they all finished high school except one, most of them attended college. Four of their children became teachers. They all work in the church services and were active members of the church and in the community where they lived. They all got married and became parents. Most of them were blessed with the talent to sing and pray also the gift to teach.

Walter and Emma Mae truly had a blessed marriage.

Today, 2011 Walter and Emma Mae's off springs are into the fourth generation. The best way to describe Walter is the Psalm 128. His life story is like psalm 128. His scripture to his children is Proverbs 3 especially verses 3,5,6. He memorized psalm 23 and other scriptures. He recited psalm 23 often upon his sick bed. His children remember the teaching of their mother and their father and also taught their children to love "Do unto others as you would have others to do unto you". This is good advice for all generation to come.

Most of the Walter and Emma Mae's children reside on Harvey circle and some of their grand children. They have built homes. Some still have horses; most have dogs and cats, gardens and hogs. No one farms any more. There are no cows, corn or cotton there are two entrances onto the Harvey circle from north side drive that will take you around the circle. Walter and Emma Mae's legacy of love live on in their children.

Walter and Emma Mae celebrated their 50th wedding anniversary with their children, family and friends. It was such a beautiful colorful, extra ordinary honorable, magnificent, fabulous affair. Everyone and everything was definitely awesome. It was well attended. Plenty of food to eat and everyone was very happy. It was such an enjoyable, peaceful celebration. They exchange their wedding vows again. The group praises of love song. The praises of love consists of Walter and Emma Mae's children, who resided in California at that time, a brother and five sisters were a spiritual singing group. This anniversary was truly a memorable, blessed celebration. Dresses were designed and made by Mabel and Odie. The Harvey brothers and sisters have continued to be active singing in their church choirs and their community choirs and in communities far and near. Some are deacons and teachers also.

In 1984, Walter and Emma Mae sold an acre of land to Emma Mae's cousin, after the children all complained about it they tried to get the land back but he refused to sell it back to them. Their daughter Mary Emma negotiated with the cousin for the land in behalf of Walter and Emma Mae. The cousin agree to sell it back (the tack of land as he had it recorded) he sold the land back for twice the amount he paid for it. Their daughter Mary Emma bought back the land for them.

In 1992, Walter requested to his children that he wanted he land to be surveyed. Mary Emma stood for the cost and having the land surveyed. The surveyor man Mr. Knight, survey the land but not according to the old pelt place. It appeared that others had claimed a portion of this land, the old pelt place. As of today 2011 this situation had not been cleared up.

WALTER AND EMMA MAE HARVEY

They shared their wedding vows in January 1932. They celebrated their silver and golden anniversaries. They were married sixty years. Nineteen-hundred and ninety-two (1992). They were in love and they shared a blessed marriage. They had (19) children, six of them died at an early age. They loved each other; she was always his "Baby". He called her baby from the time I can remember until her death. We were their pride and joy. They were always there for each other, and of course they were always there for us.

Walter and Emma Mae had a blessed family life. The best way to describe it, by referring to Psalm 128: "Blessed is everyone that feareth the Lord: that walketh in his way. Thy wife shall be a fruitful vine by the side of thine house. Thy children like olive plants round about thy table. Yea, thou shall see thy children's children." This is about how it was with Walter's and Emma Mae's family. We gave them respect and honor. Our parents loved and respected each other. Our Father accepted his role as husband and father whole heartedly. Our Mother accepted her role as wife and Mother whole heartedly. Our Mother was truly a mother in every aspect. She was always there for us. She was home most of the time. Seldom, we came home from school and mother was not home. You can believe it was serious matters of concern, if our mother wasn't home when we returned from school. She was always there for us. The scripture best describe our mother is Proverbs 31:10.

THE WALTER HARVEY FAMILY

A SPECIAL FAM-I-LY

Our family times were happy times.

We shared love, smiles, laughter's, jokes, tears, secrets, lyric, strategy, hugs, doubts, fears, aches, pains, minds and peace. We worked together we played together, we ate together and we prayed together. We had our share of happy, happy times! We wore old clothes, hand-me-downs, and new ones too. We washed our faces, combed our hair and said Grace before we ate. Sunday morning we went to church. Monday morning we went to school. We went to bed on time ad hard the cock-crow very early in the morning. We fed the animals, fowls, and the squirrels too. We had no time to be bored, very little time for television. We cried, because of the pains, but Mama was always there to help heal the wounds. She taught us to love and forgive. She showed us the way by her life style. She was an excellent mother, a loving wife, and a hospitable neighbor. She was always Daddy's Baby and we were and always will be her Babies. Daddy smoked his cigars sitting on the porch in the summer time, and by the fire place in the winter time. He always corrected our foolishness, and he did not tolerate our nonsense. He always gave sound advice, quoted "do unto others as you would have them do unto you." Later, as he got older, he quoted "lean not unto thy own understanding, in all thy ways, acknowledge him and he shall direct thy path." Their Christian teaching and examples have shown us the way!

MARY E. HINES

"What things soever ye desire when ye pray, believe that ye receive them, and ye shall have them." Mark 11:

Walter and Emma Mae truly had a blessed marriage.

Today, 2011 Walter and Emma Mae off springs are into the fourth generation. The best way to describe Walter is the Psalm 128. His life story is like Psalm 128. His scripture to his children was Proverbs 3, especially verses 3-6. He memorized Psalm 23 and other scriptures. He recited Psalm 23 often upon his sick bed. His children remembered the teaching of their mother and their father.

MARY E. HINES

OLD HOUSE

NEW HOUSE

Offspring

Mable Lee

Mary Emma

Vera Mae

Walter, Jr.

Artell

Katie Mae

Odie Mae

Spencer Michael

Ruth Helen

Daniel

Stella Louise

Webster

Sandra Marie

Walter and Emma Mae children and:

Mabel Lee Harvey-Purnell/Oscar Purnell married 10 years 6 children, 6 grandchildren and 3 great grand

Mary Emma Harvey-Hines/Theadore Hines married 48 years 5 children, 9 grandchildren, and 3 great grand children

Vera Mae Harvey-Mickles/Alvin Mickles married 40 years 4 children, 6 grandchildren, and 4 great grand child

Walter Harvey Jr./Lureatha Lewis-Harvey married 28 years 4 children, 1 stepson, 6 grandchildren, and 2 great grand children

Artell Harvey/Catherine Moore-Harvey married 45 years 4 children, 5 grandchildren, and 2 great grand children

Katie Mae Harvey-Henderson/C.W. Henderson married 45 years 2 children, 7 grandchildren

Odie Mae Harvey-Clark/Percy Clark married 26 years 1 child, 1 grand child

Michael Spencer Harvey/Verdie Ruth 1 child, 2 grandchildren

Ruth Helen Harvey-Benjamin/Samuel Benjamin married 40 years

Daniel Harvey/Liz Harvey married 20 years 3 children, 5 grandchildren, and 1 great grand child

Stella Louise Harvey-Young/Young 1 child, 2 grandchildren

Webster Harvey/Linda Harvey married 29 years 3 children, 6 grand children

Sandra Marie Harvey-Sims/Alonzo Sims married 20 years 2 children,

Second generation

Mable Lee

Willie Albert (deceased)

Bobbie Lucile

Ralph Darnell

Gloria Jenetta

Susie Marie

David Lee

Mary Emma /Theodore

Emma Corenia

Herbert Lee

Harold Louis

Joel lynn

Janee Latricia

Vera Mae/Alvin

Jerome Bruce)

Mivchelle Renee

Mildred Elizabeth

Lisa

Walter Jr. LURETHA

Orlando Marichal

Claudette

Dorothy Jane

Mischelle Renee

Ronnie Charles)

Artell/Ca6therine

Denise

Glendlyn Faye

Cynthia

Albert Lynn

Brucie)

Katie Mae/C.W

Carl Douglas

Kasandra

Odie Mae/Percy

Naomi Christina

Michael Spencer/Verdie

Trevell

Daniel/Elizabeth

Mishia

Monte

Chessica

Sharon)

Stella/George

Aaron

Webster/ Linda

Trecia

Webster Jr.

Centaria)

Sandra/Alonzo

Emily

Harvey

Third Generation

RALPH DONELL HARVEY

Ebony

Ralph Jr.

Abree

SUIE MARIE HARVEY

Sherrika

Joseph

Mable

EMMA HINES

Larry Larnell

LaStaria Markeshia

Lanee Jovonna

Theadore Lavell

HERBERT HIINES

Jaquoia Leah

Javlon

JANEE HINES

De'Shon R.

Jaivon Denzel

Da'Auna Ranee'

MICHELLE RENEE MICKLES

Summer Jenae

Derrick

MILDRED ELIZABETH

Justin

Kearria

LISA MICKLES

Laikyn

Devonte

CLAUDETTE HARVEY

Dessirree walteria

Daniel Jerone

MISHELLE RENEE

Marvelous DaShawn

DENISE .

Jason

Paul Alexander

GLENDELYN FAYE

Keshia

CYNTHIA HARVEY

Marquis

Mya

CARL HENDERSON

Caleh

Shyahana

Tocoria

KASANDRA HENDERSON

Cory

Cornell

C. C.

Katie Corenia

NAOMI CHRISTINA CLARK

Chershia

TREVELL HARVEY

Essence

Achantis

MESHIA HARVEY

Mareshia

Jasmine

Marquivous

MONTE HARVEY

Kiasia

CHESSICA HARVEY

Gabibrell

AARON YOUNG

Layla Rae

Kaya Monte

TRECIA　　**CENTARIA**

Allen

　　　　Kala　　Charles

Coby

　　　　Jaylon　　Chelsea

The 4th Generation

1st Mable

2nd Ralph   2nd Marie
3rd Ebony   3rd Sherrika
4th Jamal   4th Cierra
4th Katahma   4th Shille

1st Mary Emma

2nd Emma Corenia
3rd Larry Lonell   3rd LaStaria
4th Evan   4th marquez Matthew
4th Ethan

1st Vera

2nd Michelle
3rd Summer
4th Amari

1st Walter

2nd Claudette   2nd Marichal
3rd Daniel   3rd Nakisha
4th Malach I   4th Tomisha

1st Artell

2nd Denise
3rd Jason   3rd Alex
4th Shayla   4th Paul Alexandar

1st Daniel

2nd Meshia
3rd Marisha
4th Charles

MABLE LEE

SCHOOL DAYS 1962-63
SUMNER HILL HI.

MARY EMMA

MARY E. HINES

MARY E. HINES

ODIE MAE

SPENCER MICHAEL

RUTH HELEN

STELLA LOUISE

MARY E. HINES

SANDRA MARIE

Walter and Emma Mae's offspring's CHILDREN AND GRANDCHILDREN

PRAISES OF LOVE, 1980-1984 LOS ANGELES, CA

A SPIRITUAL SINGING GROUP, WHO SUNG ON VARIOUS

OCCASIONS IN THEIR COMMUNITIES AND HOME CHURCH.

THEY SERVED FAITHFULLY MANY ENGAGEMENTS. THEIR

SINGING WAS INTERRUPTED WHEN MEMBER OF THE GROUP

MOVED. THEY ARE; MABLE, MARY, ARTELL, KATIE, ODIE RUTH.

MARY E. HINES

TRIBUTE TO MOTHER

THANK YOU FOR BEING A MOTHER

WHO FEARS THE LORD. . .

YOUR EXAMPLE HAS TAUGHT US

SO MANY VALUABLE LESSONS.

THANK YOU FOR YOUR INSIGHT INTO

GOD'S WORD AND HIS WAYS. . .

OUR LIVES ARE RICHLY BLESSED.

THANK YOU FOR YOUR FAITH

AND DAILY TRUST IN GOD. . .

YOU HAVE ENCOURAGED US

TO NEVER STOP BELIEVING IN WHAT

GOD CAN DO.

THANK YOU MOST OF ALL FOR THE UNIQUE

BLEND OF LOVE AND UNDERSTANDING THAT

MAKES OUR RELATIONSHIP SO SPECIAL. . .

THE GOOD THINGS YOU HAVE DONE YOU HAVE BEEN

FAITHFUL, SHARING AND CARING FOR EVERYONE

YOU KNEW

Your Children,

Mr. Walter Harvey

To Dad,

We thank God for you Dad. You were a wonderful father and husband. We love you and we honor and respect you as our father. We know that you loved us. You gave us your best. Your love, your sharing and caring. Your understanding and your devotion. Your friendship and most of all your love as a father. We appreciate your guidance and generosity. You provided for us so that we never had to go hungry. The only time you were away from us were the—you were at work or busy during the day. You never left us. You took care of your wife and your children. Most of all you taught us to love and fear God. You took us all to church and you were daddy to us.

A TRIBUTE TO MY FATHER
WALTER HARVEY JR.

He was a Man among Men

A Father among Fathers

A Friend among Friends

A Speaker among Speakers, where ever he was asked to speak: He would fit anywhere.

A loving and devoted Husband for his Wife, and a loving Father for his Children.

He was also well loved by his family; His beloved Mother and Father, his Sisters and Brothers. We all just loved him dearly.

I can remember the times we shared together; Daddy would always say, "you all will never find a man like your dad. I kept money in your pockets; I always bought you nice clothes, I always kept food on the table. I made sure you all got good education. Not many men take time out with their children like I did with mine. "I still play with you all as if you are still small children". And I would say fI know daddy", you know most of my friends parents are either separated or not living.

He would sometimes say "when was the last time you hugged your dad? "; then I would say today, and give him a big hug. I will never forget the good times that I've had with my dad.

He had many friends and he said good things about them all, if there was anything they'd need help with, he wouldn't hesitate. He was always willing to help.

St. Mathews 19:19 says Honor they Father and they Mother: And thy shalt love thy Neighbor as thy self. And I thank God that I can truly say that I've Honored my Father and Mother for the years that he has given our Father to us all. And there will never be another but my Heavenly Father: And some day by and by I shall see my Father in the sky.

70th Birthday's

Mabel Lee,	September 20, 1932
Mary Emma,	July 5, 1934
Vera Mae,	March 4, 1936
Artell,	June 28, 1938

MARY E. HINES

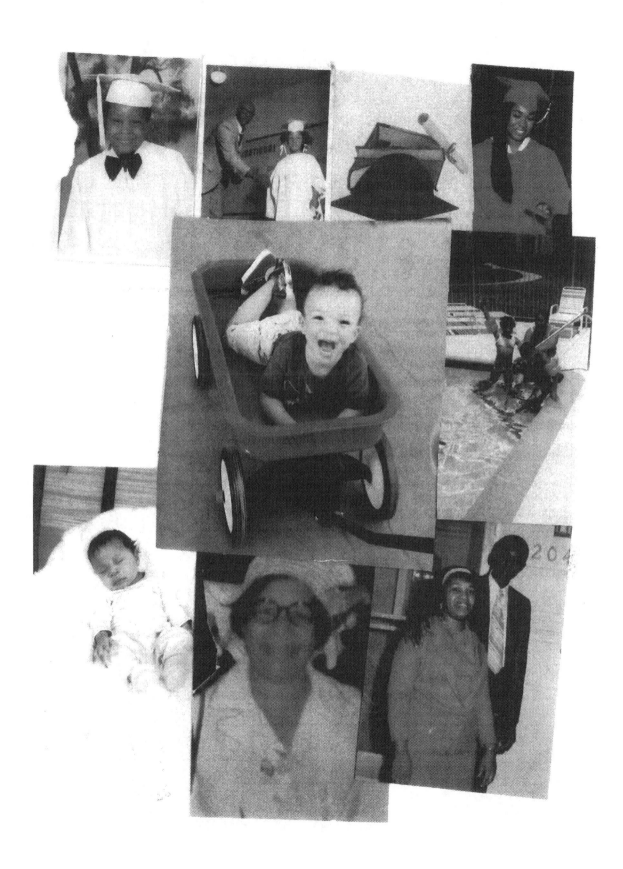

MARY E. HINES

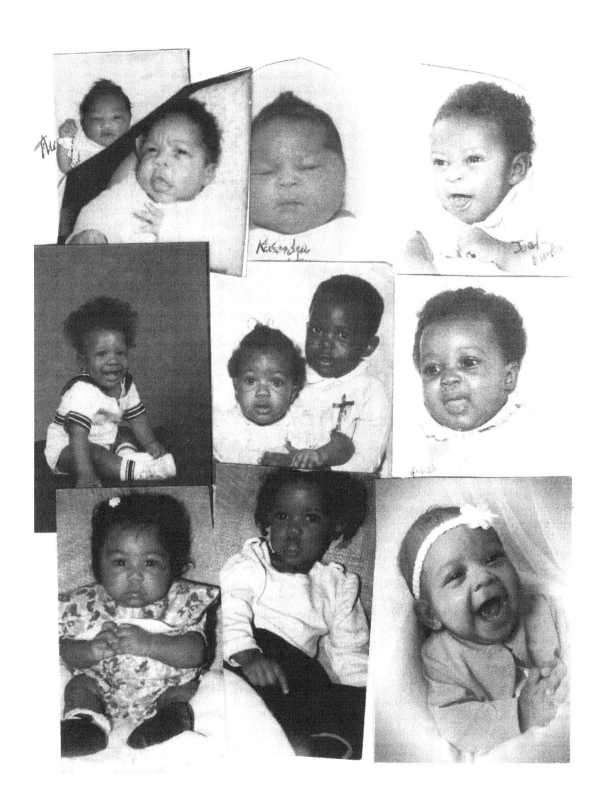

MARY E. HINES

MARY E. HINES

MARY E. HINES

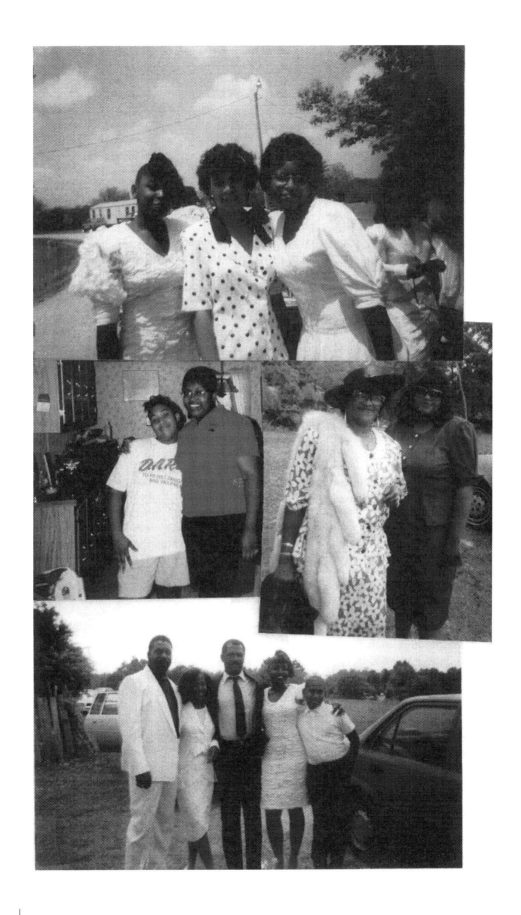

MARY E. HINES

MARY E. HINES

Shori_ka
Gloria
Maria
Bobbie
Ralph

Liz
Gloria

Marie
Emma

Shorintha
Christina
_____

MARY E. HINES

Marquez. Eaton. Evans. Emmi

2010 Harvest Festival

MARY E. HINES

FAMILY ACTIVITIES

MARY E. HINES

MARY E. HINES

Harvey Circle

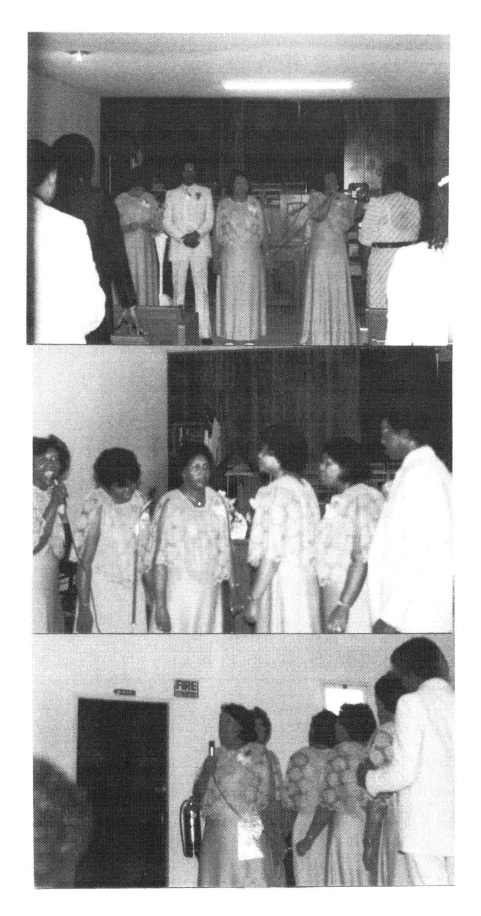

MARY E. HINES

MARY E. HINES

MARY E. HINES

MARY E. HINES

MARY E. HINES

MARY E. HINES

CONGRATULATIONS
We are so proud of you.
You made it!

MARY E. HINES

MARY E. HINES

MARY E. HINES

Honoring the 55th
Wedding Anniversary

of

Mr. and Mrs. Emma and Walter Harvey, Sr.
Sunday, September 6, 1987
at
4:00 p.m.

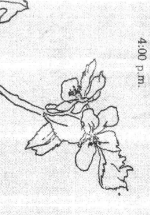

MT. OLIVE MISSIONARY BAPTIST CHURCH
West Northside Drive
Bolton, Mississippi

Rev. Augusta Harper, Pastor
Mistress of Ceremony — Sis. Mary E. Hines

Program

Opening Song . . . . By the Choir

Scripture . . . . Bro. Aaron Young

Prayer . . . . Rev. James Graves

"How Great Thou Art". . . . . Sis. Ruth Benjamin

Greetings. . . . . Sis. Kasandra Henderson

Special Selection. . . . . The Harvey Family

Poem. . . . . Sis. Johnnie Atkinson

Solo. . . . . Sis. Dorothy Huddleston

Reading . . . . Sis. Lisa Mickle

Duet. . . . . . Sis. Ruth Benjamin & Bro. Spencer Harvey

Words of Inspiration . . . . (3 Mi . . . .)
Led by Sis. Mable P . . . .
Sis. Anna Patton
Rev. John Hill

Solo. . . . . Sis. Lula B. Williams

Love Offering . . Brothers L. C. Henderson, Bro. Alfred Hopkins
Bro. Artell Harvey, Sis. Bobbie Harvey &
Sis. Estella Young

Selection. . . . . The Harvey Family

Remarks & Acknowledgement . . . . Sis. Mary E. Hines

Closing Remarks. . . . . Rev. A. G. Harper

Benediction . . . . Rev. Harper

**INVITED CHURCHES ARE WELCOME TO WORSHIP
WITH US ON THIS OCCASION.**

Nancy and I send our warm congratulations as you commemorate your 50th Wedding Anniversary. This is indeed a special occasion to be celebrated with much pride and happiness. We wish you every shared joy in the future.

Ronald Reagan

EMMA'S MOTHER,FATHER, SISTERS, BROTHERS STEP_MOTHER

MOTHER ABEL HILL JOHNSON (deceased)
FATHER LACY JOHNSON (deceased)

BROTHERS and SISTERS
KATIE MAE (deceased)
WILLIE (deceased)
ARTELL
LACY JR.

MOTHER, WILLIE

(deceased)

(FATHER' CHILDREN)
JAMES (deceased)
BEN (deceased)
CLIFTON
WILLIE C.

MOTHER; GERTRUDE WASHINGTON HARVEY EDWARDS (1948)
FATHER; WALT L HARVEY (1910)

BROTHERS and SISTERS:
ROBERT   (deceased)
ANNIE MAE (deceased)
ESTELL   (deceased)
THOMAS   (deceased)
MARY E.
GERTURE
PERCY JR.
MAGGIE   (deceased)
CARRIE BELL (deceased)
JAMES T.
JAMES C.
WILLIE L.
BETTY L.

May God Bless You

april 89 – Feb 56   Lacey Johnson (papa)

MARY E. HINES

Mamma Emma

Doddy Walt

Mary Emma

Bobby Watt

MARY E. HINES

THE AUTHOR

Mrs. Mary E. Hines, is a native of Bolton Miss. She and her seven Sisters and five brothers grew up on a farm with their parents. She received a Bachelor of Science Degree from Jackson State University and participated in her Advance studies at U.C.L.A and La Vern University. She received a Life Standard Teaching Credential in Secondary Education. She taught Junior and Senior High school. She stays busy with her family and church life. She has written several books; Juvenile, Fiction and Non-Fiction.